THE DUST OF DREAMS

THE DUST OF DREAMS

A COLLECTION OF POETRY

To anyone who has ever dreamed, anyone who has ever loved, and most passionately to anyone who has ever reached out in search of a memory.

- Sebastian

CONTENTS

SUNFALL INTERLUDE:

2:

<u>To Start</u>

I couldn't decide what I wanted to show you

All the doors to keep open or closed

Threaded shards of my heart and soul to offer

A raven, bringing trinkets to the park people with bread,

To start to learn which earns him more

A keychain heralds mystery and begs the question of doors

This is a well in me, it is a spring from my soul

A novel, and journal, and diary

Take it in stride, I'm under the pages,

And I would like your company

The Weaver of Tales

What makes you different – how does your writing

Stand out against the trillions of words on paper?

My insecurity traces nails against my spine

Tries to claim me

Own my waking mind

Breeding while I sleep

Like spider eggs

In the attic corners.

Ah, I'd love to entertain you

Maestro of my instability

But you are sorely outnumbered

Two thousand and one restless souls torment me,

Begging for a feature, a fleeting line

Their tales – unfinished business left unsaid.

I write not always in third person or first,

But in the possessed voice

Companion crows, my dreary whisperers

Third and fourth eyes wide open

Two spirits, one mind,

The Weaver of Tales.

Collecting words passing from red painted lips,

Oiling, separating, lifting ink from ancient pages

Stitching it into my passages,

Spinning out paper from typewriters,

Like cloth sweaters on a loom

Patterned quilts, a patchwork of sentences,

A hundred little moments to tell a story.

Mushrooms and Moss

Mushrooms grow where everything else dies

Fanning out from shriveled branches,

Aged gaps and cracks in the bark

Springing from grayed out irises of the poet

Wealth of life from the roots of death

When the fallen log begins to rot

The orange mushrooms give it color

Oh the moss too, a spongy swarming thing,

Out of the boulders, around faerie doors and circled stones

Over graves and forest marshlands

Traveler, welcome stillness in the clearing

A home in places only your soul has been

My dear Persephone, revealing now ephemerality

From it I've learned, and so I'll be

Still enough to let the moss grow over my toes,

Long enough to let it bury me

I Wish to Be a Ghost

"I'd die for you"

Such a noble line as this

Once passed the roundtable knights' lips

But it is not now a sacrifice

If you are already waiting to go

To live for someone gives life meaning,

But your life carries centuries

Only after you are dead.

It's a question of belief then,

That which gives life to the dead things

Do you believe in ghosts?

I've seen them

Homebound on the northern lights,

Leaning on the lamppost in the alley

Tipping their hat, knowing something I do not

I wish to be a ghost,

More powerful than a memory,

The living past and undead future,

More than a fly on the wall

Should the world burn

The Styx

Life's waterfall, death's waiting pool,

And the limbo divide – a river in between

That we spend our whole lives staring into,

Waiting for our time to cross

And hoping that in our reflection,

There is some kind of solace

Before the other side

Fearful passage marks the end of all things

It has haunted and it has called to me

And I wonder if I'm only standing here,

A stillness in the dark

Waiting for the ferryman to take me

Is there something deeper in the water than my own reflection?

There's so much gold in the riverbed, I'm sifting for the stream

There's an ice-blood bleeding down my neck

A red cloud over the sea

A pearl forms at the estuary of my eye

If I let it fall, and it takes its leave of me

What does my one tear mean to this, the endless sea?

Map of the Stars

At one time I saw the path the stars had charted for me

So I followed it, believing that a celestial path could, somehow,

Be a dyad of my material one

At the end I found nothing but stardust, lingering

Still I stood on the beach, searching

Pleading with the silent stars

Their presence gave no instruction, the map had faded

So I rewrote vows of love etched into the sand

And begged the endless horizon

Tell me why I am not enough

Though my screams were anguish filled

My cheeks flushed with desperation

Much like the stars, that distant line

Gave no answer

You Stirred Something in Me

Who taught you how to play my heartstrings so well?

Delicate harpist in my soul chamber,

Was this same music in the air

When the wind flew in from the car window

Was it showing itself in my eyes,

Is that how you knew

That you could be the bead of ink

To my clear, undisturbed water glass,

And fill it so quickly with a distraction

An all-consuming plume, that's what love is –

How did you learn to play that into me?

I want to know,

I want you to teach me

Not Quite Death

I had this recurring dream when I was seven

About what I thought was death

Family by my bedside

I never once got to tell them goodbye

As the roof flew into the black sky

An angel untucked me and pulled me into the wind

He dragged me between taxi cabs

Pulled my pale form around avenues

And set me hanging over it all,

Floating tied to earth

Over the city and its noise

Jazz street, newspapers, snuffed cigarettes,

The beyond I felt around in for a promised land

To be tethered to instead

The angel opened to me a door of heaven broken,

Everything coated in gold

Apples, rotting, a woman, frozen

Not quite death, not quite immortality

Beast in act three, *what will become of me?*

At the doorstep, I refused him,

I refused this offering, if offering it was

Not quite death, stale bread, not life

Open

      your

           eyes

                and seek it yourself

Star Trail

It seems like I always find hidden secrets

Glinting from behind tree branches

Just over the walls of fenced off gardens

In the places the universe wants to keep

A little bit of itself captured, for a seeker to find

It hid a glimmering star trail for me,

Through the light sauna made of water-soaked logs and

Hot coals from a fading firepit that warmed the garden wall

I made myself invisible, still, a non-malicious stone gargoyle

Entangled in these vines of stars

Part time observer, watching peace unfold

No one had to dwell on any cut, scuff, or scrape

I earned on my journey of discovery

I was invisible, and embracing it

Dying among the wildflowers the universe grew for me

A starry lining

Peace – to live in

Railroad

The train travelled through the morning fog

Wheels gliding across a century old railroad

It rode through the woods and into valleys,

Circled mountains and traced coastlines,

Greeted quaint coffeehouses with its sharp whistle

Connecting sky to earth with rolling steam,

The railroad took the train into forever

Until forever became the soft country night

Again illuminated by the morning fog

Olive Tree

The lowdown neighborhood was sun-dried
Hot air filled with the scent of barbecue smoke
Stained tin butterflies and glass hummingbirds
Hanging under the arches of doorways

I saw a girl, gilded in happiness
Almost floating across her front yard
She comforted and spoke to
The marble angel weeping at the pond
And adjusted a small clay gnome
Sitting at the base of the porch

The gilded girl planted California succulents
Beside a rusted mailbox
And around an olive tree in the center garden,
That looked so much like mine once did.
The air passed through its branches
With a thousand whispered voices
Rustling the leaves like wind-chimes

I still remember the shearing of those leaves
On one mid-October eve
Shocked – more than I thought I'd be

I had rarely ever climbed that tree,

But I couldn't hear its voices anymore –

I couldn't hear myself

What might he be saying about me?

A once boyish adventurer turned tired roadside thinker

I was scared to lose my younger aspirations

So I walked lightly on the eggshells left behind

From where this new me was being born

To avoid reality – the shell crunch under my heel

Then the hands of the clock fall forward

The girl needs the marble angel

To be her comforting

The olive tree's leaves grow back

To remind us how to breathe

Every newborn goes fast and gets old

And the reborn?

They watch, without a worry to wait for

Like an olive seed

That's patient for the earth to open

And the reborn live

Woodland Song

A forest does not sing with words

A forest sings with whispers, soft melodic gusts of air,

The accented gibberish of a thin creek

The rhythmic rustling of dead, dry leaves

Birds and owls providing their harmonies,

The occasional beat change of the snapping twig

Or fall of a breaking branch

It is the song of filled silence

A symphony of quieted cacophony

Lakes to the Oak Tree

I came to you in the chaos

Between the reeds and southern cattails

Life tried to thread the air from my lungs

But I breathed in the lake on which I wrote

My inspiration was the stillness

It told me I was there

And took me to its canvas

In endless meadows of flowers

Wind rustled grass, an air of peace

At the empty shore

Where the sand curves beneath waves

I knew nothing else

Ignorant bliss found in the calm

There was stillness there too

Oh no need to make waves

But if you don't make ripples

Were you even here at all?

Returning from gray sky blues

Across the rails and the cobblestone

My air restored by the old oak tree

Its trunk and roots a seat

I can't wait to write under you again

The water-soaked soil

But my mouth still dry

Green grass fields

Darling, it's been a long time

Withered Rose

Its ends are tan, crinkling like parchment,

folding into the sides of still lush petals

The stem is falling, the leaves droop in melancholy

The rose may be a few shades darker,

Absent of reflection as it dulls to black

But this is not quite a withered rose

This rose can grow again, it can be healed from its scars

Can be brightened by the rays of the summer sun,

But a withered rose is not like this.

A withered rose does not resemble a rose,

It lacks any former beauty, any precious soul

It is far more akin to the fallen leaves of autumn,

Though one is celebrated, both are dead.

A withered rose is one step away from dust,

Then dust it does become

You may have never truly seen a withered rose,

But I can guarantee you've felt one

A strange sadness you can't quite describe,

a feeling of being out of place

As if you've drifted far from your roots

A contemplation of your meaning

If you ever feel within you that indescribable wistfulness

Know that the currents of thought within your mind

Speak to the dust of a withered rose

Saturn's Rings

If I sat on Saturn's rings
To watch the universe alongside
The solar system's prince,
Would I even be afraid?

Even as my body pricks and tingles
With adrenaline from fear of falling
When I glance down, I could be rising
If I remember to forget gravity

The north star is no longer north,
There is no north out here
Only a million split directions,
A billion miles in any way

Just one of those points, a blue speck,
Barely visible atop my thumb,
And all I care so deeply about
From here, it wouldn't matter none

I can look all around me now
From the crest of Saturn's crown,
The stars are white on Earth

But take away the smog

Voila! A spectrum is revealed,

A festival of luminance,

Bright above where I stand now

(light)(weight)

A dream of floating, surrounded by

Radiant rich caramel gold, aged shining silver,

Iridescent silk blues, a lilac aura undertone,

With pink and red sparkling hearts.

The milk of stars spills and clouds this nexus in the void,

I beg, let my bones fall open on the memory foam

That is the embrace of empty space.

Maybe when I depressurize

In the airtight shuttle cabin

My burdens won't return the same

And part of me can be lifted, holding onto the light,

Cascading from the nebula

Into me

Void where all the socks go

In the folds between sweatshirts and pocket lint

There would be where I would throw

My curious little self

The void where all the socks go

Five fifty in one cent coins,

Fading tie dye t-shirts,

Childhood scent and voice

A portal only active when the dryer door is closed

There – all the things I've lost and miss

Cotton tuft trees growing leaves of forgetting

And a wonderland of pocket-sized trinkets,

For me to love in memory only

Honey and Ink

The hive in your ears,

Anxiety of the stingers

Constant, low buzzing

The wooden floorboards are alive

The lace window coverings,

Blot and draw lines through the light

There's an air about this place that speaks

Can I tell you something you've heard before?

Let it touch you differently this time

Let the words pour over you slowly,

Like warm honey

Sink in, harden,

Like amber

To fossilize the living truth

Words you've heard before

Felt, to the very marrow of your bones,

That hurt no less now

The pages frail, the books weak spined

Thicken the air with disjointed prose

Each story a whisper of paper dust floating over,

Decaying spores laying seeds of inspiration

Fair feather, find the ache in me

Sometimes, after

The ink flows far more easily

Than the tears

Candle Heart

It waited to be lit, in a thin cage of glass

And it wouldn't take much to set aflame

A warm fuzzy feeling is more than enough

To melt my candle heart

Charred wick, liquified base

Burning away, losing itself to the wind

Wax running down, veins of lost tears

Sparks flung from steel gray eyes started it

An eternal flame

Overnight on the stage

When in my darkest days it's all I have left

To keep my hands warm from a cold shoulder

Maybe I shouldn't,

But I know I'll burn for you

Until I am the last light

The Sands of Time

Returning to the beach I knew

These sands would look the same

Covered in that rare pure magic of a summer rain,

Warm afternoon sunlight, or an ashen snow

Snow?

Who am I kidding, these westward bending shores

Are not forgiving enough to hold snow

But they are greedy, and hold onto

All the little pieces of my future which I gave to you,

That I left littered there some other time

I turn at the poles above the waters

Watching short-termed visitors and idle pacers,

That will return someday to see an imagined impression

Of their own footsteps

The sand is holding history under its few hospitable layers

In its cold, clammy depths with buried things

Hollow sparks of soul standing where they did before

I did not intend on my return to see you but,

I thought I did

An echo of a memory, residual traces of your energy

I measured out my feeling wrong the day we met

I placed too much into your arms,

and watched it spill into the sand

Every time I return to that shining sunset shore

That fine, entrapping, grainy crystal floor

Blue sky and waiting, reliable waves

I see the impression I've left in those things,

facedown, my eyelashes dusted with sand and seawater

Afterimages still dancing in my mind –

you by the bonfire that night,

Salt pours into all the little wounds scabbing on my heart

In my head I never walked back onto that beach

Without flowers on the edge of bloom

For the only one I felt my soul itself had tuned to

But here I stand amongst the empty, expansive sand

No music seems to suit this moment, to bottle it, but still

Notes from a folksy guitar in the key of G

Float and find their way across to me

Gone are my favorite pastel skies of yesterday

Under cherry stained horizons that pass in moments,

Now, I lie awake and think – who will get your sands of time?

Who will leave their mark so painfully permanent on your heart?

Not that I can really stand the question long

A jealous vein in me hopes none will, that only I'll have this

Remembrance lingering of a yet unread future,

That I already gave to you

–

I came back a second time

Too late for the sun to kiss me goodnight

The mist was thrown over the shorebreak

As I was walking our fine line,

An elusive tan stream that our broken hourglass left behind

We've not been talking lately, but I wouldn't mind if you came

To sweep me back under the tide

I wouldn't ask you to

Someone will take care of me

But I'll mistake an airplane for a shooting star

And wish that you would instead

The red light flashes, out past the drop off

The ominous, vast expanse of uncertainty looming

Cold depths where no one intends to bury things

Yet never free of graves

It seemed like I was seeing out your lingering blue ghost

Without a choice

But the soft light was just the same wave breaks

Glowing, for me,

One last time

<u>My New York</u>

What you were, my darling,

My New York, glimmering light, beacon on the Earth

Heart of evergreen, of Central Park

Full of history, the shouts and whispers of the city folk

My New York, archetypal city,

To which all others are compared

The key to the ignition of my desires

Well of motivation, untapped by those yet to arrive.

The comfy couch and warm fireplace in every rainy day

And in each raindrop the beautiful colors reflected

The flame to light every shadow

Hearth's ember amidst ash and smoke

All the lonely lights

The water on the shower curtain, glossed like oil on sheet glass

Droplets scattered light from the center of the room

Through them I saw all the lonely lights

Decorative candy canes in the snow just outside town

The last streetlamp to flicker out and burst

Fiesta bulbs, strung from an 80's Volkswagen bus

A lighthouse and its ocean liner

Tiny candles, lit to guide tiptoeing steps

The lantern waved from the window of the night train

A car on the desert highway, the only headlights for miles

Each star above, surrounded by millions of miles of empty space

Each lonely light its place to shine

Each one its own battle

With the dark

Bookstore girl

Longing for the magic you made me believe in
Was my coping mechanism with time, fleeting

I stand convinced that fate and chance shook hands
So you'd find your way to me

An unwritten story in the space between novels
Young love had nothing on us

Rain on my tongue tasted of musk, aging
The sparkle in your eyes still hung in the air

Even when you were gone
When I lost you to winding streets and forest leaves

The lyrics to every song have become about you
So I write them on my heart, waiting for a reader

Moonbeams

The moonlight streamed through, 11:29 pm

It glided over the kitchen floor to meet me

T'was the sun offering me a flashlight,

While it spent time opposite the world

The silver of the moon reminded me of so many things

The way it looked last summer

When it was my only partner at the top of the hill,

Waning low in the horizon

When the only thing I wanted was to be that moon.

It was brighter than I had ever seen it

The brilliance of the sun, purified by the darkness of night

And so I bathed in the heaven light

Letting the moonbeams permeate my skin, illuminate my mind

I became a child and a wise man all at once,

My eyes danced with wonder at the sight of it,

And misted with the burden of knowing

Somber Island

You wrote this song for me

In the back rush of wind

Your soft voice complementing chords on the ukulele

My mind drifts off placidly

To a place that doesn't exist

The sky there is always lavender, and cloudy

I lay stretched between two palm trees

Just out of reach of your kiss,

In the dim light of a forever dusk

An ashwood table holds my candles,

Smoke curls in delicate tendrils from the wicks

As the ocean breeze gently snuffs them out

The waves never swell, static and calming

Oh this island is lonely

But beautiful and dangerously so

For a second

As the last of the melodies play through

I'm a fool, for thinking I get to stay

A Ripple in the River

Bent over, staring back at my own reflection

When water runs over rock,

Sometimes the river transforms things

Its ripples are windows

Tree shadow and basin clay mix

Forming images, playing tricks

Dragging me back

Night, temperate as sugar and spice

Though not everything is nice

When my mind is facing a reinvention

Love was painted black over my heart

Like the oak bed of the chariot

Your winter dress, and the dreary sky

Blue as the even' star

The lights on the country club tree

Made the leaves a shining emerald

The fire in its place was dancing

and the people followed in suit and gown

Clementine glow, the color of your distance

I reached for your hand, extending warmth

But it was never mine to hold

With truth, every ripple clears

My distorted reality resets to default

In clarity restored, the woods around speak to me

Midwinter dreams are gone, they took you with

I'm left to face a muse-less spring

As the ripple melts into the river

Glimmershore

The light on the shore waves

Dances over to me

Dressed in ocean foam white,

Waltzing without stepping time

Only for the beat of the wave.

Inconsistent diamond dancer

Who rules the ballroom

For as long as she is in it

<u>Then you came along</u>

A voice to charm the sailor from the sea

Deep, comforting, and familiar, like the last three turns home

A smile that provides more warmth than a fire ever could,

Slow burning candles and roaring hearths do not compare

A laugh to fill an empty heart

Like warm caramel drizzled into a dark chocolate shell

Eyes of storm and wistful fog

Sparkling like the dawn, beacons home like a lighthouse

A soul as rare and beautiful as black opal

Hidden deep, a wealth of secrets, a delicate gemstone,

But in no way fragile

Rarely is anyone so fortunate to meet someone

As complex, as kind, or as genuine,

While it may be my fate to lose you, my greatest windfall, truly,

Was to have met you at all

She Wrote First

The story, desperate to be known

Pages blanketed the floor, painted the walls

Lyrical and whimsical, a narrative in emotion

She wrote first, the tale of the universe

Arms of the typewriter sore,

Inkwell becoming thirsty, an empty glass

Feather pen exhausted, blunted by parchment

So she wrote with her tears, the cry of the lonely

And when the people turned in ignorance,

She cast her fury on the earth

Splitting mountains and bending forests,

Churning the very tide with the passion of her chronicles

She wrote the gravity of the moon

It was not lightning in a bottle,

She wrote and it was smoke in a shot glass

Tarnishing copper plates and darkening lace

Fogging the edges, clouding story with theme

Burning the midnight oil, to capture its conceptions

Snowstorm

Memories like a swirling snowstorm, loud,

flying at me all at once,

Beautiful in crystalline structure and uniqueness,

Yet fleeting, caught easily by the howling winds

that blow from the recesses of my subconscious

Winds laced with longing and nostalgia,

interwoven with threads of uncertainty

Oh, if only I could hold the snowflake before it melts away,

If only I could grasp the memory,

Before I forget the meaning of that day

If Evil Lays Dormant In My Bones

Repressed into the marrow

Trying to ignore that which I was

Then awakened by the screech of electric chords.

Cruelty in my past comes to haunt me when I'm at peace,

A beast of myself, knowledge that I am capable of the same lows

The potential for evil, validated by the venom in my history.

All the cyanide I dropped in drinks, the knives I placed in backs,

The demons I let out, proven by the marks they left

That still feel fresh on the chambers of my skull.

I stopped being afraid of monsters in the closet

When I realized the demons within

Were far more oppressive than any external one could be.

Somedays I am one with the bullet,

Vengeful spirit vectored down dark corridors

The pen breaks this sword into its little fragments

But can't contain the casualties woeful adolescence brings.

I put out my hands to stop you

But they've been idle for too long

Evil has crept into the calluses over my bones,

And you fell into their trap

They have minds and vendettas of their own

Even the nothing in me doesn't function like its meant to

Red Cedar

The Canyon trees below seem to be on the crest of autumn

California knows how to hide December

Behind a dry leafed and warm aired smile,

Until the cold wind passing through my ears stirs up thoughts,

Awakens perception, and arouses emotion

My scars can't hide the bitterness

I poured out for myself

I'm a dancer in the shadows where the sun hits others

I've been played like a violin, but never in a symphony

I've got calluses from those silver ribbons, but

I loved the song anyway

I fear I'll wake up one day in a

Blatant December of some colder future place

And there'll be snow, not a trace of fall

Spiderwebs of ice, frozen and fractalized

Part of me will want to remember – you are living

Though the silence-marked distance carries doubt.

Seldom are the living realized, should they not speak

To me, you'll be dead as the weeds

That hang on the roots of the red cedar

Silenced birds in a barren branch cage

Would ask if they could

How long do rotting roots stay in the ground

After they know the tree is dead?

The seeds of connection I planted are

Long past bearing fruit,

I see them curling to become weeds instead

All around me they soar,

Blocking out the compassionate sun

Within me they tangle in knots and cover my hope

Until, when the dust clears, there's none

My mind in exile from a woodland body

Red cardinals and blue jays pick at what's left of me

I'll grow reliant on the maroon sweater-clad stranger

Walking from loneliness with me

He could see my internal decay like

A flaking crush that cracks open the old log

Who had risen so far, for so long

Beautiful flames still scorch the skin

I'll fall off the tightrope if I let my eyes slip down

These are the wrong seeds

For a tempestuous being of the earth

Flower fields are curses, tight vines hurt but hold

And the dust of my dandelion-seeded dreams

Drifts off to where nothing grows

By the fallen red cedar

Elsewhere

I'd find myself in cornfields

In husk and burial mazes

Trimmed bush and petals

The red rock mountains would look so sweet

A passage to escape, to the other side

Space to breathe,

Where the red cedar is standing now

SUNFALL INTERLUDE

Glass Shattered Forth

It started with looking up

At something,   a light that shined

It was almost blinding, though not sun in the moonroof

Fireworks,   a man-made celeste

Over the four lane, filled with masses of glass and rubber

Stars: Now in Color!   bursting, a shocked audience

New eyes, satisfied, dip down too late

Looking over,   an empty passenger seat

And the speedometer needle was straining

Rotations rolling   'til they screech

The way made free, high, with speed

All the headlights froze   the sparks a shower

Glass shattering forth, the car spinning, *did it ever*

My body flying   through the windshield

With shards round me

Floating there,   tiger stripes on my cheeks

To bleed the last time, with a pleading sigh

Don't eulogize me, love me while I'm here

It ended with not looking

      Anywhere

At all

And I am reminded of Sunsets

There have been moments

In this time I've had

That have been so full of life

They put whole weeks to shame

Made months of monotony

Pale white with emptiness

The color of the morning dew

That struck me on the pink rose

The gold sparkling firework

That lit the fried powdered web

Of the strawberry-topped funnel cake.

The lone beach and I

The shore's hand on mine

Every sunset that crashed

Into the horizon

And broke the locks of color

To let it fly out and paint the sky

Could I eat the moment like the cake?

Can it fill me so and sit there still?

Can it linger on my clothes

From when I rise, like dew

Can a hand on mine that's there

Not leave, for a while longer

And may I sit and watch the sun

As it breaks the lock

So that the purple rolls in

Over my head

And the bright red orb sits

Only half below this edge of the world

Saluting its tinted parade

So that I may bathe in this saturated light

And nurse the drink of it

For the next month or so

Truth or Dare

Where's your vulnerability, what's your sacrifice?

One of body and mind, the other heart and soul

Beneath red veil and parlor tricks

The shadow man, in his charisma, offers dealings with the devil

The only ones who ever win,

Are those wise enough not to play at all

Tell them the truth, and let it all play itself out

Or dare to take the low road, and give in to the easy way out

It's dangerous, there's a craving for it, a desire,

Thinking thin wires are enough to hold us together,

And pulling them to the breaking point.

If your sadness is playing fast and loose with fate,

Then what's the point?

I question, like a dice roll, a minted coin toss

Coming right to the edge–

Hold me down.

A desire to be freely lost doesn't make it sound

Nothing ventured is nothing gained,

But what is never risked is never drained

Greek Grapes

I felt the birth of a nation on my tongue

Present for its conception and its fall,

A youthful feeling that you know will age, refine itself,

Like the wine of the priests in sacred gold cups

Fruit to grow was meant to wait

Greed cuts the vines and plucks too soon

Discard, don't heed the warnings, he'll say

And eat the thorns from an iron hand

Blood runs down at the corners of a two-faced smile

Fills the cracks left in the fountain

Marble statues to tyrants of eons past

Put them all up on a pedestal, whilst we just fall

Enticed by spiraling, so glorified and fictionalized

There's almost a longing for it

We enjoy being engrossed in our tragedy

Gifting grapes to the iron handed, holding fate above our head

These things are cruel but comforting

Yet we stay fearing what change will bring

Replacing the marble pillars on the crumbling temple

Be sure not to rearrange the order

Stagnant – one more thing will then remain

Enamored in our graves

All our kissing skeletons will look the same

As theirs did

<u>When it Rains</u>

You can feel the rain coming
Ionic air is tensely pulled
A static sheet beneath grey skies

When the clouds begin to open up
Raindrops fall and hit the window
Like feet pressed on piano pedals

The song is Spring
The house wood creaks, breathing
The piano sings, just shy of sleeping

Lulling waves in the pebbled air,
Stoplights in rainy eyeglasses,
Droplets racing down the sullen street

The streaks paint clarity with opaque drops
As God's foot shifts the melody
Notes changed in length, richly

For rain was never His tears

As hopscotch-playing children once told me

But a sheetless music

Washing the soul

Rain – God's great symphony

Ashes Where the Tea Leaves Should Be

The house only looks right burning

If it's to stand without you in it

There are labyrinths of dead space in me

I wander through them as I sleep

Too many things I didn't say out loud

I'm cursed to never know the way out

You were my Eurydice

I know looking back was the greatest mistake I ever made

My mind is too quick to make the future a memory

To create a history of what now won't be

Is there anyone out there?

I'm still at this table, an empty cup alone

And there's ashes where the tea leaves should be

There's ashes where the tea leaves should be

Can my appetite for love be sated?

I try to keep on giving

But so much has been taken

I still have the tattered cloth

I wove together from the scraps of you

If I gave you every piece of me

How was I so easy to remove?

There's ashes where the tea leaves should be

There's ashes where the tea leaves should be

My mind holds onto your knuckle bones

That I cast like die

That I read like braille

With a tender touch

Red wax drips down, so hot it burns every love letter

That it was meant to seal

Twist my arm in a twist of fate

When you reach for my hand

Is it me you hate?

Where were the omens when you said

Don't stay

And I did?

Place your head over my pillow heartbeat

If you can rest this once

I'd like to claim I gave you peace

Before I claim that I feel free

I fear I can never be

I'll be shackled to this memory

When you fall asleep, I lie awake in these dead leaves

The ashes blanket my bed sheets

The chip in my cup remains

And there's ashes where the tea leaves should be

There's ashes where the tea leaves should be

All the things I could not say

Seem to have been spelled out here already

Time approaches our withering tapestry

And it always buries me

Spring

When hot, one has undoubtedly wished for a cool breeze

Gentle equilibrium has always been the human desire

Yet, though I am wishing for summer,

The biting winter winds do not knock at my door

No, now it is spring, or so I am told

But what is the measure of a spring without rain,

without roses and without butterflies,

without the smell of new air?

I have lost touch with these, for I am trapped

Behind papers and books,

Screens, a digital fabric of reality

Barred too by concrete walls,

Though they all say we are placed within those walls

To learn of life outside of them

Well, when summer comes for me, all this will have passed

Yes, I wait for summer,

So I may yet experience the spring

The Poem Says

The poem says

The light is always fading

The smoke is always just dissipating

Gold is hollow, empty

Found by a fool for its shine.

The only ocean I could swim in

Is one of my own tears

In blackest night and brightest day

I see two different mirrors of a self

And it's in the quietest hour

That the most trivial things

Seem to roar with meaning

Lightbulb

Hours broke the lightbulb finally

Spiderwebs of cracks stemmed

From the ends to his base

The inner glass smoky, stained,

Differently from glass in the church

Stained by the dissipation of light,

Afterimages depicting his former warmth

A conduit, broken by the pressure,

A light, dimmed by overuse

Exhausted, and out of his time

Where We Are

Wake up every day, same places, same people
Is there something in monotony?
Is there just a wait for it to be gone so we
Search in all the little things,
Building out the houses of our dreams

When the air changes scent and weight
I understand the necessity
To move out and take in a breath
When the same words and tired things,
Hang long in the air, it seems
Like this moment is all we are owed
And we want more than we are owed
Though at times I've stayed in a chair for days, unmoved
I've learned more about the world than a skydiver would

He thinks if he finally sees the curve of the earth,
It'll make up for the time wasted,
Not feeling the grooves of his own tree's roots in the dirt.
We are a generation of lost discoverers
Who think the road itself can rebirth us–
Yet we fail to look twice where we walk.

Give the passing wind a chance to feel your hair

Talk to the stranger,

And fear – not what grasps the moment there,

But the regret, if you never take leaps where you are

Intangible

Nothing physical is as built to last

As we may like to think

Our screens will crack

Our pictures will fade

All the things we "own"

Will crumble and dust

We place so much meaning on material

But our clothes and jewelry,

Papers and trinkets

Will all rot and rust.

We only have what's in our hearts

And touches our soul

We have only love

To give and take,

To cherish and to hold,

Our most valuable possession is love

In all its many complex forms

In the end,

Even when someone who loved us leaves

The love they gave us never does

It has created us, changed and built who we are

And truly, only love can do that

Real, honest, open, loyal, unyielding love

Of a parent, of a mentor, of a friend, of a partner,

The love, even, of a stranger

Nothing we can hold affects us quite the same

The most real things in life

Those that last, that stir belief in the hopeless

Conjure forth feeling from numbness,

The boundaryless things that connect us

Are those that are intangible

Daisy House

There's a road through the mountains in Southern California

Surrounded by the forest, sprinkled with cabins

Most are traditional, iron fire and log composition

But one stands out near the crest of a hill

The roadside Daisy House

That I saw on my ride through

Daisy House was painted blue, with yellow framed windows

Pots of flowers growing out on the side

A clover grass bed in the garden's place

I saw a lady outside this house as I drove idly past

She had been crying, I could almost trace the lines on her face

But now she smiled at the sunrise

With her back to a willow tree

Her back to what had passed

You will, too, no doubt, find at some point

That something has tapped the faucet of your heart

Your cheeks, too, will know tears as a washing

And you may wonder how you will ever escape

The hole it seems you've dug yourself to climb in,

Facing a burial of your own past

Then one day it might be

As simple as sitting under a willow tree in a sundress

Letting your hands spread open

On the brown-sugar earth

Feeling that the seeds are growing,

Bursting forth in a morning stretch for the sun

And rising to meet you

Launch Point

Leave behind waves in a rush of dust

And shoot toward the cosmos

Looking out for stars,

Admiring cotton candy clouds collecting mist

As you pass them on your way

Break through the wispy ceiling

And hover – just where there is space to

Perched amid a pin pricked obelisk dome

The lights below are something like

Casino machine slots, gold, red, inviting

In a tempting way

Or maybe they're a thousand parking lots

Streams of highways

And pools of darkness

Which may not be void of population

But appear void from here,

Up around so much infinity

Past the hazy ring of light pollution

Obscuring it before

Sever gravity's ties with lifted spirits

Letting colors transmit their vibrance through your soul

And fall back onto the pillowy layer of sky,

Lit up from beneath by city lights.

As Apollo drives down the sun chariot

And Ra begins his nightly journey through the underworld,

Settle with the sun

Sunfall

Dawn marks a different day,
By noon though, its true colors have begun to show
As the sun dips and we enter the night

The prevalent night, marked by hate,
And haunted by death that conceived it

Questions asked in the darkness
"What's going on, where is the love of yesterday?"
Born of the fact that the beloved sun has fallen

Descent into disunity below the dayline.
Thousands of mothers tired of watching their sons fall,
Forge and steel our motivation.

I will not idly watch the sun fall into devil talons
Fire from my fingertips will light the keys
If that's all that I can do

We have marched, arm in arm, down the horizon road
And we will hold up the sky, share what Atlas bore,
The color of our united voices will be what means more.

As long as love runs through us like a luminous trace

We will never let the sun fall.

2

Winter Town/My Escape is a Fantasy

Christmas lights pinned, hanging from the eaves,

Beneath the snowcapped roofs of warm homes and antique shops,

Sparkling from the windows of the diner

A picturesque holiday card

A sad, but beautiful place, dusted with snow, like fine sugar

Full of cinnamon spice, hot chocolate, nutmeg and candy canes

Cautious travelers on the icy roads

Warming up with fresh chili at Maury's

Kisses meet half numb lips and chilled noses

People of all ages watch their breath form in the air

Daring to stick out their tongue and catch a snowflake,

Standing in the middle of Main Street

Between holiday cheer and seasonal loneliness,

The soul sits, an open window to his back

Snow is blowing through the window shutters

The log fire stoked in front of him is popping and sizzling,

Like buttered popcorn on the stove

A blend so contrasting and yet perfectly paired

Not even the best ice cream scoop in town could compare

Teeth in cookie dough vanilla, as cold as rosy fingertips,

Sticking out from hand knit gloves

Leather couches covered in blankets and winter jackets,

Christmas crackers filled with Polaroid film and tinsel.

A 60's record scratches to life in the other room,

Muffled notes, bells, violins, and grand pianos

Tales of magic, love and chance, Santa Claus and elves

Here no one is quite alone,

There are friends they've known all their lives,

Each constantly pursues their own moment

Underneath some fictional mistletoe

Hanging from an endless expanse of multicolored skies

The Fortune Teller

I met a fortune teller at the county fair

Under red-white tents and moonless skies

Off the thrill of roller coaster rides

I don't know what I sought from her

Maybe it was the first letter of my soulmate's name,

An affirmation of my dreams,

Perhaps I wondered what she could tell me

That I didn't already know,

Would I listen if I heard it all again?

She saw dying forests and empty beaches instead

The purple fog of her crystal ball faded to a lusterless silver

And she told me I was better off sleeping, so I did,

In my dreams I was chasing the dead, and the dying

Ivy walls and pearl rain, all this and the golden ghost

And I saw so much does die,

Youth, innocence, memory, self

All this death, society calls a cold case,

Fearing it will be prosecuted

I met a fortune teller, and foolishly,

Forgot to ask for lies

Walking Willfully into Melancholy

My back to the sun in early afternoon,

My destination lies in the dark clouds and rain ahead of me

I thought darkness to be my melancholy

But it must not be, because light is not all pure picture

The sun still shines on headstones

And clouds darken the daisy.

What makes the passing raven any less of one

When he picks his rodents from the sunshine?

What makes the hummingbird any less of one

When he drinks his nectar under a heavy shade?

Darkness and light are temporary

Creatures from both sides even the scales when out of place

The yin and yang make balance safe

But reality is in their blended gray

Life is not all lamp light or shadow cowl

A house ahead, with string lights hanging from the fence,

Buries the thought that warm light

Cannot make a home in darkness.

So here I am, walking willfully into melancholy,

Knowing it does not make me

Packages

I know we'd like
To round up the years in packages
Our pains, sorrows,
Changing moments, even our joys
To clear our slates,
Write elegies to the parting year

Take our lives and sum them
All tied up neatly in a bow
To be gifted as nostalgia
When the dust is blown off

But time moves like a river
On which we simply drift

It carries silt from upstream
The realizations, changes,
And yes, communal pain
Personal pain
From its journey before

You can never step in the same river twice

But if you float around for long enough

You'll find it familiar

Try as you might

You cannot package your life

Do not waste your one river journey

Trying

In the Mundane, There is Still

Room of glass, a warming hotbox

Afternoon, that hazy hot non-summer

Makes the invisible tangible

Time is heat, and burning

Dali illusions waves on the blacktop tar

Melting clocks, the slow down rush

Silver streams of water

Bead and race down the street

Like gallium in the glare of the sun

A curtain of sand dust pools up with a whirl

Lemons life was doling out

Are now mostly in my blood

Seed gum eyes stuck staring

Down like melted wax

On creaking floors

Like a daydream

The Novel

On my bookshelf I have a novel
I loved since I was young
Today I went to pull it, dusty off the shelf
And it was heavier than I expected
As if a wire at the back resisted my hand

I hoped briefly that there was a room behind my bookshelf,
That would jump open and to life
A secret society meeting place
With crushed mint and lemon berries
In empty jars of strawberry jelly

Atlases of explorers, their old-fashioned copper compasses
Pressed wildflowers and lilies plastered on the walls
And a thousand secret books, with locks for ornate keys to fit
That held all the secrets I may have died without knowing
Secrets, that were shared once over black and white tea,
The lucky few that made it to ink on the page

Alas, the empty gap

Looked only at the wall

And so I opened up the novel, and searched its worn pages

For all the secrets I might have missed

To satisfy the fearful craving in my heart

Mooreville High

Summer's end meant midnight reunions on the track
Still rubber permeating the air in the heat of August
Friday night rumors and tailgate daydreams,
Parties with the rich kids and songs sung in the backseat
Peering over the hedges lining the football field,
We popped confetti and shouted, "Go team!"
But loved the moment we shared more than them

The one winter, when snow fell on our little town
Prom in the gym was so beautiful
Dancing lovers nestled under a flakey powder blanket,
We watched as the disco balls made stars of the spotlights
They highlighted the love affair, we traded envy for laughter
Fruit punch sometimes stings or leaves stains
But we drove out in our gray sedans and felt like royalty

We'd hide by heaters at the Barnes Crossing mall,
Ride the carousel, race security on the way out.
If the school staff had been careless, there was a small chance,
We could sneak into the theater and gaze up at the light fixtures
Didn't worry much about making it back home
Breakfast at the coffee house, lunch at the diner downtown
Resting on the bleachers when the evening sky rose

I won't hold on to what I won't miss

But I'll certainly miss skipping service at the Methodist, with you

Fast friends, and young love, the pain of growing up too soon,

Driving away from the schoolyard singing made it worth it

Worn souls, the cruel cold, friendship lasts until the bracelet breaks

Our hearts can only carry the fire of youth for a little while

So I'll leave our innocence and beautiful ignorance on the page,

So that they may fade more slowly

Tchotchke Ring

This was another poem about the sea, romance conspirator

This was another poem about you

Though I tried to promise I wouldn't write those anymore

This, is about a boy,

Who bought a ring with a copper colored band

At a trinket shop near the edge of the suburbs

A boy, who thought his girlfriend might like it because

It wasn't formal like silver, or boastful like gold,

But sweeter, and nicer, and younger, like them

He marveled at its tiara shape, and let it rest atop his finger,

Counted out nine plastic diamonds, eight days before Valentines

Took it home, and boxed it up, reminisced on 7 months

In six days, at five pm, he sat alone at a table for four

The only one they had left in the diner

He ordered three milkshakes while waiting,

Barely finished the second one before he left

He was up until one am, one day before the day of love

With one tchotchke ring, and no one to give it to

So he threw it out into the street

And it rolled down the hill, stuck on a storm drain

Till it was found by me.

Sensing its story, I gave it purpose once more

But a curse is bound to repeat itself

Storm drain removed, it still found its way to a whirlpool

As I cast it out into the ocean

Though it was meant for another girl

A younger one than the sea

One whom I loved, one whom I love

Oh

so

fatefully

The Witches Tree

Gnarled branches twisted in a ghoulish catch

Wire brush stumps stemming from the aged trunk

Sap bubbling and oozing from a cauldron-shaped knot

Bleeding heart on a sleeve, outstretched fingers, not for me

Someone left behind a hopeless enchantress

To spin branches around her raven hair,

Cast her eyes of earth into this hollow

She took a love potion for the sun,

She'll bend to him

Forevermore

The Ocean's Burdens

She has seen much.

Pioneers on a weary journey, hope in the prospect of new land

A child, desperate, his cry for help all bottled up with a stopper,

Cast into the future by her rolling tides

The faces of sailors streaked with sea water and sweat

As the storm rolls in above them, and the winds relay their fury

Passengers, accepting a fate they could've never imagined

Their fortress of iron keeling over, saluting the sky

Drifters, waiting for a passing ship,

The right lighting to shine out a beacon

The desperate and hungry, the fearful and tense

The rescued telling their stories on the beach years later,

Those whose stories end on the open water.

Lovers, writing their names in the sand

Waiting for the waves to sweep away what they wrote

She is entrusted with these things each day as the tide changes,

Love, lives, journeys, and messages.

The Lovers

Fateful afternoon, well met were they.

Sunflower girl with the midday glow in her eyes,

circlets of stars tattooed on her thighs.

The lady, the mystic, pink-blue unicorn hair,

sharp jaded eyeliner, a cutting stare.

An unlikely pair, warm fields to dark garages,

evening churches of sacrilege to gold gilded temples.

A love, the best of both worlds,

holding to the light golden rays in late afternoon,

stolen moments in the dark between the candlelight.

Juliet and Rosaline twisted in the bedsheets of fate,

when they pushed each other on the swing set

A little higher and I'll grab a cloud for you

Questions and a kiss,

the neon monsters watched them,

no space between vests of studded green lights.

When the kisses were light, but no less amorous,

lightly folded between moments of graceless kitchen dancing.

Their love was spinning over countertops,

trying not to knock over the saltshakers.

Their love was growing older, emulating the other,

Predispositions present in paintings and piano pieces,

Veteran spirits of a time when their love was outlawed

The deck drew the ten of swords, the eight of cups,

Doomed right from the start, and at every step

Death could not but bow

As their heartbeats slowed and matched

Dual circadian rhythms uniting.

When they died they both saw it coming,

Faced it together

Left together

Lover's hand

in lovers' hand

<u>Same Sky</u>

And to think

We've spent all our lives

Staring up at the same sky

Sure, the clouds may form thinner here

I see Orion as you see Scorpius

But we've both seen rainfall

Known the beauty of a golden yellow morning

A deep red orange sunset

The harbinger of night

Your head hits the pillow as mine rises

The sun dips below my horizon

Giving way to the moon and stars

It rises into yours

Celestial bodies take their final bow

But for a moment at dusk

A second at dawn

We feel the change together

We see the same sky

Dusk in San Francisco

Dream in the steel blue

The house of rusted metal by the pier

Lightly salted, crisp air

Breathing across iron supports

Bakery bread mixed up like wet concrete

Concrete kneading itself like dough

Tawny tan green grass paddy, unkept

Dancing, bending, double-back fire escapes

Broken brick on the old buildings

Streetlamps and telephone wires

Glow and spark, frizzes of light

Cerulean coated sky, dipped in a cobalt evening

Fading pinstripe clouds

Potted sunflowers and lemonade

Bell hanging lavender and warm tea

The Golden State and the Golden Gate

Red at their dusk

Woman at the Window

Her back was turned, face hidden

Arm resting on the rosewood table

Teak, woven cardigan, pulled snug over a vintage t-shirt

Her auburn hair, wavy and full, matching the colors in the table

Turquoise stone earrings, with speckles of gold, dangling beside it

Sitting comfortably, draped like a blanket just over her shoulders

Blending into the ornately carved cherry wood around the window

Framing her face, just off center, a dimly lit silhouette.

Outside, beyond the dusty windowpanes,

You could still make out clearly a single cedar tree, near the house

The rest of the forest blended – an evergreen canvas

Fog hung over it, caressing the treetops

The breath of morning had clouded the window

She traced a cursive message in the mist

What did she see, what did she say?

Curious mind, eyes of wonder, curtained by auburn hair

Hummingbird House

A red door swung open, the porch dust stirred

And my young eyes danced over it all

The white picket fence, shaded gray clouds in the dark night

Grassy lawn, illuminated by the soft moonlight

I saw you there, a bright smile I had only seen in photos

Too young, I didn't bottle the memory in the meadow

A sacred place

I truly can't remember if I dreamt it

But if I try

I can still see fireflies that kept the tree lit

Golden – like my grandmother's vibrant soul

I know better as I'm older now

I know she was the one that opened the door

The hummingbird zipping through the larkspur told me so

Sugar water dripped from the feeder

Just as sweet as not knowing

If this was a dream or a memory

From your heart to my hands

If this snapshot is not truth, I understand

But if it was a dream, I didn't dream alone

Spiderweb

Today I walked right into a spiderweb
It caught on my teeth, the frizz in my hair,
It laid on my eyelashes and crept into my nose

When I finally managed to splutter it out,
I wondered about another moment
When I might've caught the spiderweb
Before it caught me

If the light reflected just a moment earlier
If some puddle that wet my shoe
Caused me to be late to this misfortune
That had been laid out almost carefully
By so many moments that came before

I can see all my other selves
Who made a different choice
Each wove a spiderweb of their own
A myriad of decisions leading there
They validated their what ifs

And for all the changes this surely brought them,

At every fork in the road of life,

I think they manage to get tangled in their own spiderwebs

The Grass in Mistvale

Rose gold rays thicken the mist
Wavy grass alive by air
Plays guitar strings and synth keys
Calls the child out of his bed.

Deep mind, fantasy is flying
The nook, growing moss on shale
Drips, the waterfall is thin
Beads fall and collect like
Caves grow spikes, slow and down.

Tracing our fingers through the reeds
Pulling at them like shimmering
Strings off nylon balloons
That soar, running now, like us
And the fountain within our blood.

Our backs on the green and dew
Heavy breathing shifts to
A chuckle and laughter
That the trees share.

Little Things

It's the little things about a person

The accent that hasn't faded from certain words

Even after years gone by

The way their nose scrunches up

And eyes water slightly

At the bittersweet awakening coffee brings.

The overlaid shapes in their pupils

And the way they see color

Miniature designs painted on their nails

With flowers and runic messages

Lip slightly curling under top teeth

As they wander their own thoughts.

Their handwriting

Telling a story,

Emulations of parent's signatures

Finer points taught by teachers

Rougher edges refined by years of shaping

Loops of practice, ease and familiarity

On every letter and card sent to me

It reminds me of all the other little things

Helping number a thousand ways

In which I miss you dearly

Refrain De Lune

It didn't take an orchestra

For you to move me

Just an empty living room

Chandelier sparkling overhead

Shuddering, not at the wind

But at the notes

Echoing through marble pillars

Ascending the corkscrew turn of the staircase.

In every rest, and small spacing in scale,

And each time your fingers touched the keys,

It was like you pressed your hands

Over the bruises on my heart.

I winced at the bluntness and simplicity

Of something so complex

For when the piece does not fully envelop the mind,

It leaves room for conversation

Between the notes

And the heart

Bridge Built to Burn

I am like the spark to tinder

Laid over cotton

With me a fire starts

But I can do nothing to keep it burning.

I called myself the ignition,

Scintilla to lovers, spark over a logger's pile

But I am just a destroyer.

The messenger often gets shot

So I avoided the bullet just in time

For it to hit the gas chamber and blow up in our faces.

I'm not a conceiver but a killer catalyst

I do not make fire, I leave ash

Where once a palace could've been.

My subconscious is the flint,

That partners with the steel of my forked tongue,

As if to say

"If I cannot have love,

then others must have none"

Girl of Smoke

She slipped through my fingers, left a black shadow stain

Incense spilling from the burner

Coals disturbed and flashing a final ember

Produce a night star curtain veil of a girl,

Smoke – that fills the expanse of a broken accordion,

It wheezes and has holes in its lungs,

And a shorter breath, like mine,

Cut in half when I catch your floating eyes

They don't tell you

that a ghost's touch feels so much like

How static sounds,

if it was a little warmer

Or maybe that's just how a memory feels

Because I'm not nearly lucky enough

For ghosts, or girls of smoke, to be real

Night Fever

I spent some time in a cabin where the fire was dry

It got so stuffy up there at night

Suffocating heat wrapped tight around my head

Like a cotton blanket with its corners stuffed in my mouth

Artificial heaters melted the chocolate

And all the ice cream left out of the fridge

Soupy, like the canals of my brain

Flushed with a hazy night fever fluid.

In a moment of mercurial reprieve

I stepped out into the mountain air,

I hoped it could freeze my brain back together

But the night fever was stronger than that.

I buried my head in the snow, to fight this hot messy thing

Emerging from it, a frostbitten child

Surrounded by woodlands that opened up, facing

An idyllic iced lake so undisturbed it reflected the stars.

In a breath my night fever cooled, for a moment

Regal beside me stood an elk, the cosmos in his eyes

He took me under mountain passageways,

Where the light at the end of the tunnel was a ruse

A trick of my thawing night fever mind

Between the frozen slopes and alpine arches

Over the summit,

Descending – forever

Behind My Eyes

Ticking clock at the back of your mind,

Something is coming.

A forewarning in our DNA,

Impending doom.

Underlaid and ever-present,

Swinging pendulum,

It haunts us to our tomb

When I close my eyes,

My eyelid's pinkish flesh is a movie screen

I am met with the overwhelming.

Conch calls a mountainous tidal wave,

A furious hurricane, to wash it all away

A blue flash of energy across the clouds

Takes my memory, tearing open the sky,

Like a piece of felt, fragile, now frayed

A supernova that lights the night, self-proclaimed sun,

Binary stars crashing into each other,

Gravity only keeping them in perpetual motion for so long

Returned here against my will

I see the orb of pure light

I reach for it, the center of the void

Drawing from my fingers energy, soul fire

Touch, a bond, magnetizing me to the eye of the universe.

Amidst the collision, between man and the eternal,

The ancient everything that possesses the orb,

I see the ink that never made it from my mind to the page

Lost words and emotions that only exist in theory,

A what if of what was.

My outstretched hands try desperately to steer the wind,

To puppeteer time and space, make myself master of my own fate

The hair on my arms is stiff, neurons pulsate

My blood, charged, limits of the body tested

As my mind wrestles with the very universe in its entirety

Questions fear their own answer,

Power knows its weight.

Surges of energy arc out, vibrating the cells in my fingertips

My blood, molten now, threatens to destroy me too

Doors close, veins open, the web of the cosmos copies the mind

In the afterfire of the touch, it all bends in circles, melds

Everything

Too much to fit behind my eyes

So I invite the wave again

Circuit

She is her father's daughter

She has her mother's voice

Gold thread tied around both of us

Squeezed at my heart tight.

Every laugh and smile

Was a centerfold in a copper wire

Pain makes art and pain makes it so hard

When the buck stops just short of breaking

And the circuit that connected us

Dies and fizzles out

It started with an electric covalence

Holding both of us in magnetic dual orbit

The eye of the storm watched the lightning fall

But now it's just a sparking cable

Dangerously close to a gasoline spill

A tragedy waiting to happen

A sharp division where there once was

A beautiful coalescence,

Wishing on the times we never said die

Cause time takes from all of us

Our circuit might be dead

But the blue current still runs through me

Even if the energy flows out

To nothing.

If I could stop time at the moment

Where electricity connected her and I

I would live in it forever

Just to feel the currents of my love

Once more connected.

Alive.

<u>The Sun-faced Moon</u>

The waning days of summer
Dangerously imperfect little bottles of time

Shredded cheese off the turning wheel
The hardened residue of waxy streams

What once was fire roasted is now
A memory to the tongue, an oak and ashen aftertaste

Smoldering coals saluting a coastline
That drips blood red with the death of a solstice

Summer is a moon with seasons of its own
It's thinning from its fullness now

Writer's Block

Yesterday is empty.

The caw of the birds is almost amplified

By the fact that I have nothing to drown them out with

Muddling through the static to make a picture

My thoughts try to tumble down the rabbit hole,

To catch a glimpse of the other worlds, but none show themselves.

Rubber screech of the windshield wipers again pulls me out of it

When I'd like to eavesdrop, the words are muffled and distant

But now when the only thing I'd like to hear is the silence,

Mumbles become sharp needles and blaring horns in my ears.

I close the door and lay on the floor to stare at the ceiling,

My blank canvas in which words appear

Then, even the traitorous silence makes a sound,

Blocking every creative dream that would've come to me

The rain-washed skid of the tires holds me from the muse's pool

Against a steel wall of resistance,

Within the total suppressing darkness

No light but the trick firing of neurons to compensate

No choice but to let the pulses of my mind guide me out

Legacy

My great grandfather

Used to walk the streets of Puerto Rico all day

My mother tells me all his stories now

Everyone knew where Juanquino was,

Buying candy for the playground kids,

Doing odd jobs and fixes in the neighborhood

Always on the move, much like me, she says

These stories I'm told are his legacy

What is a legacy?

It's screaming out into the not-yet-existing,

"Remember me!"

Living in such a way that you stand out

Among the branches of a future descendant's ancestry

Wondering – are all their legacies woven into me?

Or am I just the next thread

In the rope that is our history

Mirror Ball

Tell me how you saw his eyes in mine

Reflecting everything you put in me

Twins share a look, twin souls share a laugh

You can catch my memories

Flitting between my fingers and eyes.

If you listen for long enough,

You can hear a mosaic of every voice I've heard

A vocal, phrasal underchord

Lingering on the precipice of my throat.

Every taste that treats my tongue was tuned

By aromas and garlic spice from Mamá's cooking

Learned to love by absorbing it

Hopeless romantic for all the cinematic things

Roll the windows down, and belt the anthem out

Close the shutters, and let the silence in.

All the little frames are filled with people

I'm prismatic, 100,000 reflections

A piecemeal soul is prettier than it sounds

I am half everyone I've ever met

And half of me

Shines forth from them

Moving (On) Day

Walking away from you feels like moving day

Cleaning out my shed of memories and poetic schemes

White walls

White lights

Bare floors

Which seem to have been cleared of even dust

The air between the door and my bedroll seems colder now

So hollow, purposeless, empty

For a second the spare sheets felt like Paris

City of lovers, lights soft as buttered croissants

The heating fan in the corner feels like

Your head on my chest

Habits are so hard to break

I can't be around heating fans and flames

They're like the temptation of a pill bottle

Hollow craving of the wine glass

The fire's heat, your phantom arms

Still wrapped around my shoulder

I'm so tired of missing, of wanting

I need a rest, for just one night,

Could I curl up in the dark circles under your eyes

Fall asleep, watching the glassy planetarium ceiling

Will you show me places that only exist in your mind

Then if I must move on, at least I'll have a takeaway

Beauty aching now, that I'll write about someday

Sirens South of Heaven

Heaven's no escape from echoes the of my past

Promises to haunt my waking

Like flowers rooted in the atrium

Of my dying garden heart.

They break through a golden mold

Stemming and blooming from the arteries

And melt it into a river flowing south

From where the calls sail out to me.

Water's moon, an illusionary lighthouse

Captains and cartographers lost in the fog

Death's song is melodious, love tempts the broken

They all die at the Siren's temptation.

Sweet harmony, strong undertow, a brittle, rusted anchor

I hold myself above the surface

The whole world my oyster, but what would it be like

If I were to open it, and find no pearl inside?

The Star Says to the Angel

You are the moon that orbits closely round my heart

You are my ride into the sunset

The jasmine smell lingering on my clothes

The breath that I need

And the only oil I've found that dissolves

Old stains I can't seem to rub out myself

I see you in my wildest dreams

And yours is the last face I hope to see

Before I fall into every sleep

Rose petal fingertips on my cheek,

A Cupid's bow that already shot an arrow through me

You make falling feel like flying

And when I call you mine

It's really just my way of saying

Who could I be but yours

I Give to the Page

I give to the stars, the ocean, and the forests, because they listen,

Because they are among the few that understand,

My turning heart of stone held in hands of glass

I'm lending my voice to their ears again

This, my letter to them, sent out finally

Penned slowly to let emotion in, given to the page

People have always said I was an old soul,

For different reasons than I feel like one

It's a curse and a blessing, a weakness and a strength

Now when my first gray hair stands out in the silver mirror

I think, *finally*, you show yourself,

Are you bringing true wisdom with you?

I sure hope so, I've been trapped without it far too long.

I kept the lightbulb that broke because it was wonder,

The candle that smells like rain and books in fall,

And a thousand other things, because I couldn't keep time

In my limited wisdom I know the time and memory on these pages

Are more permanent than the ink

I often find myself wandering around the neighborhood,

Window shopping for a different life, *would it then be a better life?*

Trying to absorb and see the best of it all from others

Moving in slow motion to get a better view of the world

I fixate on my movement and see nothing at all.

It's hard for me to remember names

Because they're so heavy when they end up settling in my mind

And my brain can't take the weight of threads

These thoughts I hold like ropes,

They tie themselves in knots and are my

Beautiful binding entanglement.

The lament of the greats is a song in me

In weaving yesterday I lay out the cobblestones ahead

I ride metaphors like trains,

Taking me one stop closer to whatever home is

Sometimes I start a sentence and hope

I'll find the end of it along the way

I think back on all the times I've held my broken mind

And found sprouting dreams amid the decay

I think I've finished

I think it's done

I think this might be over

Ready to turn this chapter's page, because

The dust of dreams is awake in me

All the hands that dropped mine to the side

Are at my back, and in my mind now

There's a shared realization between you and I, dear reader,

Every moment we've ever lived has led us to this one.

I know the end, and that there is only now

So I'll keep giving to the page

For both

Polaroids Among the Sunflowers

July days empty you of adrenaline, too much time to think

Lemonade tangy at the back of your throat,

The ocean in your chest, as you try to fall asleep

Summer puts her hand over you, to calm a churning heart

Rolling hills of light give way to silhouette mountains

The beams in the window are orange in the late afternoon,

Every eve is purple, before my feeling fades to blue

Pictures roll by on a slow film reel behind my eyes,

Like the slow nostalgic turn of the rotary dial

My head is softly shaking on the bus window

Driving to a lush sunflower valley

Silky air, light enough to pass, just present enough to be tangible

Salmon tulips in the snow, a beautiful girl

Standing in flower fields

If winter ever touched a moment here

Thousands of white framed moments come for me all at once

Blinding lights on the pier and in the stadium

The kiss of the waves and a last embrace

Golf carts spinning and songs for the skies

A rush of instantaneous ink and toner paintings

I arrive between my mountains

Under the billion stars that know me best

And among the sunflowers, who shield the lakes of memory

Seeing storms, love in stages of "almost".

My toes touch the earthy soil

Rich with the salt of the sea that sometimes still rolls in me.

I know as I hope in endless meadows,

These polaroids belong among sunflowers

That'll love, entwine, and shine on them – forever

Acknowledgements and Author's Note

Thank you to my mother, and her dedication to me. Who pushed me off the precipice of "I want to be a writer!" with the truth, "Then you have to write!"

Thank you to both of my parents for being an incredible sounding board during the editing process, and always my biggest fans.

Thank you to Isabelle, Ella, Katie, Devin, Emma, Emily, Julia, Sarina, Bella, Dani and everyone else who lent an ear, a helping hand, and encouragement that helped push this out into the world.

To Stephanie and Giacomo, I hope you enjoy these writings as much as you once said you would, and that the anticipation was well worth it.

To my brother Gabriel and my dog Maverick, for giving me the gift of time whenever I said, "I was thinking of working on the book tonight, actually" (Which was often).

And to the one who heard these poems as half-baked ideas, in late nights and midafternoons, who would listen as I expounded upon every small detail that I managed to sneak in. Thank you, it meant more than I can ever express.

Dear Reader,

I've been waiting to write those two little words. Sometimes it feels like I've been waiting to say all these words my whole life. If vulnerability is a memory, if it's a story in emotion, if vulnerability is why we dream, then this collection is that kind of vulnerable, and I needed it when it came to me. Like these words, dreams offer this sense of escapism, while at the same time offering a startling, and often unexpected reflection of your own life through their exploration of your emotions. That's what writing this collection felt like to me, at least in part, granting inspiration for its title. I can't truly express in full what these poems mean to me, and how writing them changed me. But I can say that I hope it sits on your shelf fondly, for some time, and that some part of you found solace in some part of me. Thank you, truly.

Made in the USA
Middletown, DE
20 September 2022

10374660R00085